On Earth as It Is

On Earth as It Is

Poems by Dan Masterson

University of Illinois Press *Urbana/Chicago/London*

Grateful acknowledgment is made to Rockland Community College,
State University of New York, for a sabbatical leave which enabled
me to complete a portion of this collection.

⊕ *The Orb of the World, a twelfth-century Roman view of
Earth. The circle's largest area is Asia. The horizontal bar
represents various bodies of water, including the Black and
Aegean seas and the Nile. Europe and Africa are divided by the
radial Mediterranean. In medieval art, the Orb is often found
in the hand of God.*

Library of Congress Cataloging in Publication Data

Masterson, Dan, 1934—
  On earth as it is.

  I. Title.
PS3563.A83405   811'.5'4   77-28380
ISBN 0-252-00663-1
ISBN 0-252-00664-X pbk.

Acknowledgments

The author is grateful to the editors of the publications in which the following poems first appeared:

Analecta: "One-Eleven Grape Street"

The Barataria Review: "The Man Who Steals Thumbs"

Bitterroot: "The Veteran"

The Black Warrior Review: the major sections of "Rescue"

The Chowder Review: "Reunions," "The Bequest," "For a Cook Probably Gone by Now"

En Passant: "Recovery"

Esquire: "Shrapnel"

The Georgia Review: "The Survivors"

Jawbone: "To My Patients"

Jeopardy: "Trinidad Sunday"

The London Magazine: "Jail-Bait"

The New Orleans Review: "Cook-Out," "An Ending"

The New Yorker: "For a Child Going Blind"

The Paris Review: "Missing in Action," "To a Doctor Who Would Not See Me," "Whatever You Say, Henry"

Poet and Critic: "An Earlier Summer than This"

Poetry: "The Outing"

Poetry Northwest: "Blizzard"

Poetry Now: "Private Room," "The Circuit"

Raccoon: "The Tower"

Shenandoah: "Legacy by Water"

The Smith: "Another Weekend"

Spectrum: "Clouds Undisturbed by Human Things"

Transition: "Seed"

Yankee: the first two stanzas of "Rescue," printed under the title, "The Fawn"

FOR JANET

without whom

nothing is possible

Contents

I. THE SURVIVORS

For a Child Going Blind 3
Missing in Action 5
Shrapnel 7
Recovery 9
The Survivors 10
Capudine 14
Seed 16
Private Room 17
Jail-Bait 18
Rescue 20

II. THOSE LOST

Legacy by Water 25
Clouds Undisturbed by Human Things 30
Trinidad Sunday 31
Another Weekend 32
To My Patients 33
To a Doctor Who Would Not See Me 34
Diminishing Compulsions 35
The Man Who Steals Thumbs 36
Thumb, Hands 38
The Tower 39
Ward Seven, Bed Three 41
A Room with a Bath 42

Bed 43
At Midnight 45
The Circuit 47

III. ON ATTENDING A LECTURE ON CRUELTY 51

IV. THOSE MOURNED

Blizzard 59
Cook-Out 64
An Office with a View 65
Reunions 66
The Bequest 67
One-Eleven Grape Street 68
The Veteran 69
Old Drummer in the Poorhouse 70
Handing Over the Cabin 71
The Outing 72
An Earlier Summer than This 73
The Plumber 75
An Ending 76
For a Cook Probably Gone by Now 77
The Elders 78
Whatever You Say, Henry 80
Stones 83

The Survivors

For a Child Going Blind

I have awakened her
when the sky was at its blackest,
all stars erased, no moon to speak of,
and led her down the front path
to our dock, where we'd swim to the raft,
finding it by touch
fifty or sixty strokes from shore.

And sit
listening to things, the movement of water
around us drawing us closer, a hunched
double knot of child and father
hearing all there is to hear,
close beneath bats who see without sight,
whose hunger is fed by darkness.

The neighbors see her often in the woods,
on hands and knees, smoothing the moss
where it spreads in the shade, marvelling
at the tongues of birds, the stained petal
of the dogwood, the vein of color
skirting the edge of an upturned stone.

This morning she awoke to the first flash
of the magnolia, and will save the petals
as they fall, their purpled lids
curling white on the lawn.

We meant to tell her how the rainbows come,
how they close into shadows,
how we would be there nonetheless;
we meant to tell her before
they arrived at supper this evening,
rimming everything in sight.

She wonders if we see them
cupping the stars, the kitchen lamp,
each other's face, and we say
we do.

Missing in Action

The thud always awakens her
where she sits at the living room window
gathering a shawl tight at her neck,
her fist a pale brooch,
its veins hard and swollen.

She has heard it every night
since he went overseas:
the muddy jeep backfiring at the curb,
his flag-wrapped body bumping to the ground,
stars flicking light on the hedges
as he rolls toward the house.

Her cane finds the corner of things
and she makes her way to the veranda door,
its screen speckled with bugs
lured by the pantry light.

At the top step
she shakes her stick at the darkness
and mutters a private curse;
she leans on the railing and takes
each step as it comes, swallowing
quick gulps of air and straining
to see the lawn.

On down the walk she goes
to the far side of the hedge
where the streetlamp lumps its shadows
on the leaves.

She pokes at the bushes and calls him
in the voice she used above his crib
three wars ago, pleading for her bambino,

expecting to see him young and warm
in his bunting, longing
to feed at her breast.

She unbuttons herself to the waist
and probes among the brush,
disturbing nothing but a squirrel,
stiff in the leaves, the mouth
dried open in its fur.

Shrapnel

("Out-patient 04066066 continues to experience frequent
nightmares concerning actual presence of inoperable grenade
fragments considered migrant and minimal . . . surfacing
particles have been removed by patient without incident.
Request for psychiatric consultation granted. DJM, Maj, Med;
16 My 71, Con Gp II US Army Corps; Dix.")

He is barefoot in the creek again,
wandering between his house and the next,
not fully awake from dreams of grenades
blown orange.

Clad in summer pajamas, he fondles himself
for slivers unable to rust as they rise
from the streams of his flesh: grey hairs
refusing to bend.

He enters the tunnel beneath the road
and squats there; the cannon of his voice,
reaching both flanks, commands the neighborhood
to take cover.

There are no replies from the ranks;
the years have covered them with grass grown wild
in memory.

His fingers continue their search, sensing movement
within, and succeed at his left wrist
where a steel pricker stands rigid
—a miniature soldier—the point of its bayonet
piercing the skin for escape.

He draws at it with his teeth and feels it
give way; with his prisoner pinched
between finger and thumb, he crawls with the current
toward light.

Caught in the death of his squad, leaving
only the moon as a guide,
he questions his victim, frantic to learn
the invasion plans of those left behind
to drain his heart.

In the blur of morning, he watches his enemy
twist once before curling dead
in the palm of his hand.

Giving him now to the stream, using a leaf as a pallet,
he kneels to the dead man's voyage.

Recovery

Drawn by a distant warmth,
the Monarch unfolds herself
from the silk of her sleep
and stumbles the length of a branch
before learning to glide
to the darkened window
of a grey-stoned building
silenced for the dying.

Unaware of glass,
she floats through it
and settles on the gentle rise
of a wrist where pale tubing
weeps within a threadlike vein.

Lashes flutter mildly like wings,
and the butterfly goes to them,
landing softly on the bridge
of the nose.

She discovers her own image
reflected beneath the lid,
and passes through the eye
to find the soul's wick
flickering in the last
of its shadows.

She fans the darkness into light;
cold ashes whirl away to memory,
and the tip of the child's tongue
drifts like a leaf
to taste the sweet dust of wings
fallen iridescent on her lips.

The Survivors

I. CATHERINE ANNE HANLEY

They knew scarlet fever when they saw it,
and they saw it on her neck and arms,
could feel it in the pulse she gave off
as she lay in fever on her bunk twisting
the blanket to her face, a headache
wishing her back to Dublin, to her own
bed, her own window where the breeze
brought the garden inside.

In three days it would be her ears;
in a week she would let go
of her fourth winter, her parents' faces
blurring away, her sisters' eyes turning
into stars as she eased out of pain,
wrapped in their blankets, surrounded
by everything she'd touched, swirling
with her in a weighted sack, to the floor
of the Atlantic.

II. JAMES EDWARD HANLEY

They were told to return to steerage
where they belonged, but stayed,
the father's eyes ending any argument
on deck; a tanner by trade, his hands
were mostly leather; the arms, massive
as country fence posts, curved
around his family bent at the railing
in prayer.

In time, they asked for more blankets
and took the children below,
where they lay broken in the first grief

they had ever known, their mother close
to the father, speaking in whisper,
learning again that his strength was only
partly his own.

III. LAURA MARIE HANLEY

The child's third night was fitful; at dawn
she awoke in chill; by noon the headaches
began, the spots scattered themselves,
and the countrymen nearest her bunk
turned their faces to the wall.

They were five days from shore; the hospital
could save her; fresh vegetables and milk
would be waiting, clean linen and gargles,
warm baths and oils when the peeling began;
she was less frail than Catherine, older,
and had never been sick before.

IV. ELIZABETH CARROLL HANLEY

She would bring her daughter through;
after eight weeks of living in stench,
eating like beggars, sleeping in straw,
they would be in America where Uncle Patrick
held a parcel of land in their name.

She would see to it that Laura Marie would be
with them; she would wager her life on it;
through day and night she stayed
with the child, keeping the others away,
restricting her diet to soft foods, listening
to advice from the curious and bereaved

Until her own eyes burned, even when shut; her throat
closed beyond words, and she lay back
on her bunk, rubbing away the strawberry rash
that was forming on her arms.

V. LIZA, MARY, AND KATE HANLEY

They stayed below with their father when the men
took the others, the men in thick masks and gloves
who said kind things to the stretchers they carried,
and told James to come back in six weeks, that all
would be fine by then.

In three hours, they were on land, walking ahead
of him, trying not to fall down in the crowd,
feeling his hands urging them on, steering them
wherever the signs told him to go, his voice
telling them all the things they wanted to hear.

A man with a badge gave them white cards to hang
on their coats; their common code, Han-14,
would get them together if lost; on to the end
of the ramp where doctors worked in rooms
with ceilings as far back as you could lean; a man
just ahead had his card torn in half and chalk
scrawled on his sleeve; they took him
out a different door.

They held hands outside and followed their father
to the trains; once aboard, they felt sure of things
and fell asleep, leaving him to watch the buildings
give way to trees; by morning, they were there.

VI. MRS. JAMES EDWARD HANLEY AND DAUGHTER

A prayerful six weeks passed slowly in the house
in upstate New York, but the time came to bring
the rest of his women home; he would travel alone,
leaving Liza in charge, and Mary and Kate
would obey her as they would their mother,
or he would know the why of it.

The trip to Ward's Island was long, but he ran
the gravel road to the hospital, stopping
out of breath at the desk to be told
the third floor office would have that sort
of information; it did:

Two entries. December, 1850, six days apart:

      Cremated due to contagion
    Elizabeth Hanley, age thirty-four
    Laura Marie Hanley, age six

The road to the depot was spotted with snow,
his hands raw where he wrung them, each knuckle
white at the bone.

The last car was empty, its windows heavy with soot;
he saw trees hardened with ice, and a sky going grey
without clouds. He pulled the shade to the sill.

Capudine

He'd learned to survive,
but lately had taken to staying on
after his nightly novenas,
to kneel slouched in the front pew
to stare up at the dead man
screwed to the windowed wall
and think fondly of the grave.

He half-expected the body to move,
the flick of an eyelid,
a twitching thumb, a groan
rising from the throat, maybe
even a word, his name, something,
anything he could hang on to.

They took him that way;
before he woke from his trance
they were peeling off his socks
for a black wad to jam in his mouth;
he felt his shoes dangling
around his neck; saw his undershorts
soggy in the baptismal font,
his cassock a costume for the one
called Sonny, the soutane sleeves
flapping as he whirled away
to the loft to slash the bell-rope
and watch it fall: a stricken snake
coiling on the wooden floor.

They cracked him to his knees
and bound his wrists behind him,
lashing them hard against his feet,
causing old prayers to form on his lips
to be knocked away by fists
pulling steady on the rope they'd hurled
over the center beam.

And up he rose to the plaster face
where they left him upside down
to circle the air, blood dripping
from his nose, his stole of shoes
bumping the silent chest,
its painted veins swelling in votive light,
his own beginning to pound
in his temples; the gathered candles
bunching his shadow on the stationed walls,
heavy breathing and a strangled voice
blurring in his ears, lost
in the slow dark turning toward dawn.

Seed

I knelt at the stump
and kissed its inner circle
before standing to undress:
the sandals of vine, a robe
the brown of aged trees.

I saw an open place
where my lips had been,
like the mouth of a chalice.

I felt its width and depth
and went to my hands and knees
for twigs and bits of earth
and dropped them in the hole.

I scanned the forest
and lay across the stump,
my body balanced, shaken
by spasms that left me limp.

I arched my back until my hair
met the soles of my feet,
the trunk fused to my abdomen.

I felt my hands rise,
fingers fluttering
in a green blur; my head
bursting into growth,
hair trembling to leaf,
flesh curling into bark;
bird songs filling the air;
a rush of wings
sealing my lids to sight.

Private Room

They've allowed her to stay the night,
to sit in a metal chair
and guard her husband's sleep,
to watch the gauze darken at his throat,
the hole in his neck
rising pink around the rim.

Sometime near dawn, she leaves him
and heads for the double doors
at the end of the hall;
once inside, her fingers fly
over the operating table.

On the floor
she crawls in small circles
about the center of the room;
she is sure she will find
the patch of skin they took.
She will know it by the stubble
left on the outer side
when she shaved him hastily
herself this morning.

When she finds it, she will go to him.
She will hold the wafer up to the window,
up to the cleansing sun;
she will lick the edges and secure it
to the sides of the hole
healing open like a nostril.

Jail-Bait

Barebacked and handcuffed to a post
in the village square of another country,
he is about to be short-whipped a dozen times
as she stands with her father who insists
on pressing charges under Canadian law.

She looks younger than she did last night,
but older than the sixteen years he now knows her to be;
there is time to remember it all:

The swarming goldfish
looking more like orange peels thrown by workers
years before the quarry sprang a leak
filling itself to the brim, leaving a train
loaded with rock to rust on its tracks
now blurred far beneath the raft
gone lopsided by his weight.

Before he was dry from his swim from shore,
she was lifting herself aboard, tanned and untouchable
as any goddess rising from the sea of a dream.
A fish nibbled at her toes, and he shared her surprise;
they propped their heads on their hands
and talked for the moment it takes to know
that there are no words.

Lying together in the dusk, he ran his hands
through the water, teasing the fish, her fingers
finding his, her arms wet still and warming, her back
stretched like young leather, softly oiled,
her legs straight out and inching toward his until
they gave heat the length of his body.

They slid from the raft and swam in silence
to the farthest rim where the pines had spent years
preparing the shore.

He lifted her weight and laid her down at his side
to watch the fish pucker their mouths and turn
from his fingertips, her eyes explaining that she'd been
where he wished to take her, and that she knew
he would make it seem that she'd never been there
before.

The only way out was the way they had come,
back across the dark water, talking unheard, alone
—the beach long empty of swimmers.

The squad car was perched like a cat in the dunes,
hidden, until its white eyes opened a path in the sand.

Barebacked and cuffed to the post, he can see
that the short-whip, curled loose in the sheriff's hand,
is as tan as her legs set off brown and bare
against her father's creased white slacks.

Rescue

A fondness for birch trees
found her poised in a patch of shade
where the wind stays broken
and the ground holds damp
in a lingering fog.

Her flared nostrils steamed
as each sound cleared itself
in her mind; it was here she learned
to live-out the seasons, waking
in half-sleep to her own bleating,
rising from the residue of a dream
that has her leaping a cliff,
falling it seems forever before
impaling herself on a branch,
blood blowing like the rapids
that roared up at her, until she wakes
unharmed, unsure of things, even
the grass where she lay.

It was no dream that brought him to her
in the midst of that frozen lake,
four mongrels yelping from shore
where they gave up the chase, the doe
sprawled on the ice, her year-old blood
leaking from a leg snapped in half
when she leaped for water and found it
gone, landing on something harder
than the paths she'd known through woods,
her good legs spinning her crazily
toward the center of things.

The ramshackle door made a raft of sorts,
and he skidded to her side, working a rope
for a noose; her sound was that of a child
shaken in the night, the eyes stunned open

in disbelief, the voice rattling
through the windpipe, stopping in time
to be garbled by the lips.

He told her things she had to know,
how the rope would seem too tight, how she
would bound on home before the morning
even spent itself away.

The noose settled about the neck and sent
a shudder down her back; he moved
as shadows move—his hand ungloved
and gliding toward the leg, tangled in rope,
to set it free, to let the tug-o-war begin.

But she had other plans, her eyes tight
on his, a new sound snorting from her throat,
her lunge crashing short against the door,
giving too much weight
for such a mild-wintered lake, and the world
gave out beneath them.

It was then he knew he cared only
for himself, his wife on shore, his children
at the window, their grandmother talking
his death away from an earlier grief still
thundering in her soul, his parents far
at home, their phone readying itself
to ring-in the news of his drowning;
those friends feeling the Sunday air changed
about them, the reason less than an hour off.

All that, beyond reach, where he stood
shoulder-deep in the shallow hole
of a broken lake, climbing the brittle rim
only to have it cave-in, dunking him

as often as he tried into water colder
than he ever imagined water to be, knowing
he would faint dead away in it, to sink
where he had floated warm in the sun
of past summers, alive as any man had ever been.

And then, as though in dream, he saw his wife
closer than before, a rope in hand, the lake
splintering beneath her, risking all she had
to risk, her eyes meeting his in prayer,
the rope whirring toward him, a neighbor lugging
a ladder, gambling his weight and age
on the groaning surface, the long pull to shore,
the doe left behind for those with boats
to axe their way and save her, only to find
her needing more than they could give,
hauling her past the crowd, to the inner edge
of her woods to die—to take a single slug
below the ear, her blood run out too far
to claim, the freeze too deep to thaw.

Section Two

Those Lost

Legacy by Water

He stands, greasing himself
for the hardest swim of his life,
the jar on a log, its cap
fallen upside down in the sand,
flicking splinters of sun
on the house, all but hidden
in the dunes, where his wife,
his son, his daughter lie drugged
from too much summer.

If they were to waken
to the quick licks of light
playing on the walls,
they would find him hip-deep
in the sea, listening to the bell
tolling from its buoy, marking
the first leg of his journey.

He turns and waves
to the empty windows, ignoring
the pain lumped hollow
under his arm.

He takes a last look
along the shore and sets out
through water colder than the lakes
he grew up in, thicker somehow
and darker, even the sand
ribbed like a washboard
seems closer as it deepens,
his long arms churning the surface
as though he were back home
in the faculty pool, matching
stroke for stroke with his office
mate, far more than the game of it
pushing them on to the tiles

and back, head over heels in turns,
neither admitting to keeping score;
his record growing worse
during the last of winter
and all of spring.

He can't help looking back
and sees the roof silent and dry,
its shingles shrunken now to one,
suggesting the pace he has set
for himself; he slows and stops,
allowing his legs to settle
beneath him, the buoy in sight,
a few more football fields away.

He imagines throwing a pass
and watches it sail the distance
before striking the bell, breaking
the steady beat of it, the gong
making the water tremble;
he feels it across the shoulders
and down through the groin.

The water on his lips tastes
more like sweat than he remembers;
the mouthful he takes, the same
as the gargle he used as a kid;
he swirls it about
and spews it out like a whale,
lying on his back, wishing already
for a glass of water; better yet:
bourbon and water on the rocks,
all on a foam tray he could push
ahead, all the way out.

He laughs aloud and takes
to sidestroking his way awhile,
easy, almost like lying adrift
in his father's arms, learning
to float from his fears,
knowing vaguely his need for water,
the clean full feeling he has
whenever near it or in it.

With every pull of his hand
he can see the buoy,
left hand passing its measure
of water on to the right,
the right scooping it on to the feet,
smooth and steady until
the boredom of it all starts
to get him, as it always did,
those long hours
in the high school pool: lap
after lap, the lungs lasting
longer than his patience.

In front of him are terns
searching the waves for breakfast,
diving straight into the sea,
disappearing to rise empty, now
and then a fish small in their beaks;
eating on the fly.

No boats returning yet,
no one insisting he climb aboard
and tell his tale of shipwreck
and survival, no one ready to believe
he could swim from shore.

On his back again, right, left,
reaching far overhead and out,
feet doing their work,
leg muscles loose, no sign of cramps,
no fatigue; left, right, left,
just like the old days
in the senior aquacade, the fancy moves
showing style and endurance;
he tries them all: the glides,
the circle rolls, the egg beater,
ending in the butterfly,
both arms jacking him out
of the water, his shoulders
feeling the strain, too much,
the sockets grown rusty.

He treads water and finds the buoy,
closer than he thought, and decides
to race the rest of the way;
one gulp of air and he's off,
slap after slap, breathing
only when breath is gone;
he gives it everything he's got
left, glancing ahead,
keeping his sightline,
the bell louder and cleaner
all the time; he glides
the last few feet
and touches the casing, barely
able to hook his feet in the rings,
his fingers tight on the seam,
and squints back toward home.

He begins to shiver, convinced
he cannot return, that the change
in his marrow may never be known;

he hangs on and weeps, pronouncing
over and over the names of those
waking on shore without him.

He closes, at last, his eyes,
the taste of blood draining
from his gums, a trace welling
in his ears, almost
aware of the bell tolling
softly tolling, as he slips
back into the sea.

Clouds Undisturbed
by Human Things

Two geese joined at the neck
refuse to go the other's way
and become themselves
and then doorkeys
in search of locks across the lake.

An arrowhead has missed
the dog's spine
blown sky high
and scattered among fish
and one prehistoric bird,
thick-winged and silent,
owning the sun.

The long-limbed fox is opening
a kangaroo's pouch drifting
ever closer to a turkey,
one leg kicking
at a possum in pursuit.

Off to the west, far from fox
and dog, fish and geese,
the crab with transparent pincers
floats after the wingless sparrow.

Trinidad Sunday

I am a beachdog dragging my notebooks
empty across the sand.

The palms are hung high with vultures;
they are soundless, these birds,
hunched and wary of any living thing,
save the dying.

They have blisters for eyes, and helmets
of grey skin wrinkled about the head.

Patient, they wait to dress the trees
with flesh torn hot from those
left dead in the tourist sun.

Memory is full to boiling;
I have come too far not to rest
awhile, just a little while,
in the dazzled shade of Maracas.

The leaves move as though flexed
by muscle; they dip
like the heavy shadows of wings.

Another Weekend

In the middle of the yard
he sits on a bench
and bangs his fists
on the picnic table,
pleading with closed windows
to "call the cops call the cops
call the stinkin' cops."

Children from adjoining lawns
come closer to see the beer cans
jump like toads, leaving puddles
that spurt under his fists
like the spittle of dogs
shaking their heads.

He goes on banging and sobbing banging
and sobbing, flailing his arms
at the children, searching
their blurred chests for badges,
their heads for hats, their hips
for guns—something, anything,
to save him from the banging
of his fists.

And now his wife appears,
strutting like a matron,
to unlock the garage, to crank-up
the mower, to drown him out
with a full tank of gas, driving
the children back where they belong,
where parents crane their necks to see
her tightening her circle, roaring
closer to the beer cans leaping,
the fists falling and rising, the mouth
howling without sound.

To My Patients

Please do not call me at home
or expect me to drive to yours
at any time of day or night.

When you sit here in my office,
please do not smoke or tear
items from my magazines.

Neither talk to my receptionist
nor whistle, hum, stomp or tap
to the piped-in music.

When your name is called, move
quickly to the appointed room;
do just as you are told.

When I enter, be prompt about
any complaint you may have; do
not attempt to amuse me.

Listen to what I have to say
so I need not repeat myself;
then dress, taking all belongings.

Please stop at the desk and pay
your total bill in cash; checks
are not welcome here;

But you are.
I hope you are feeling better;
come again when you are not.

To a Doctor Who
Would Not See Me

I passed your office six times today
wanting to turn up the broken walk
and slip inside to wait at the coat rack,
hoping your nurse would say: well
as long as you are here I suppose—

But I only looked in, recalling
your leather table and knives, feeling
the lump on my arm, rubbing it
hard to make it go away.

You will find this note when you come
outside and will check the back seat
and floor for me and drive off
in the dark, your mind racing, your wife
alone at home, miles away.

Picture me now, my breath hot
on your kitchen window, my eyes
sweeping over her like a tongue.

Diminishing Compulsions

Uninvited
and unannounced, obsessive fears would take his head,
causing him to whimper for hours, doubting
the diagnostic measure of his curse.

He grew unsure
of the restraint they said he had by the very nature
of the malady that seemed perpetual in its motion,
as though a sack of unborn spiders had absorbed
his brain.

He was afraid
he might do things, strange intricate things, bizarre
as a web would be if found spun across his open eye.

As a child
he'd touch the handrail twice on the way down cellar
to keep things even and never once stepped on a crack
because he feared the certain breaking of his mother's
back.

He was well
into his twenties before the vile thoughts began forming
on the crust of the sack; it took years for them all
to die.

But now
it is mostly the past twitching like the leg of a spider
will do when pulled from its socket awhile before it dries
to dust.

The Man Who Steals Thumbs

From the bus stop he goes straight
to the closest hardware store;
he likes hardware stores, always has;
something to do with the iron and wood
of the place: hinges, bolts, axe handles;
nice to touch, to rub.

He fondles a work glove and lays it aside,
enjoying the smell it leaves
on the tips of his fingers.

He reaches a back counter to find
three types, but sees at once the pair
he needs; they have short rubbered-grips,
and in the crotch, just above the connecting bolt,
a circular section, a half moon
on each blade; when open, the mouths
gape at each other.

He hands them to the clerk and waits
for the change to come back across
the thick wooden slab worn grey
by a lifetime of Saturdays.

He leaves the store and crosses
against the light, stuffing the empty bag
in a litter basket screwed to a pole.

His mind goes prickly, as it always does
in new towns, this close to action;
he palms the cutters and walks the three blocks
—nodding as he goes: here to a shopper, there
to a child on his bike, an old man rotting
on a wooden bench bolted to the sidewalk.

He slows his pace at the walkway, takes it
in stride, and enters the vestibule, moving
respectfully to the parlor on his left
where clots of mourners ignore him.

The rhythm in his chest picks up, his mouth
dries out, he kneels—crossing himself alone,
and takes what he has come for.

Thumb, Hands

Its nail needs trimming
but if I pull the scissors
from their case I will surely
ease them in under the nail
spreading a sleek white path
back through the quick

A week ago I slammed it
in a door it pulsed
and bled in my mouth

Last night I lay for hours
with it tucked under its hand
flicking it out from hiding
to flex it adjusting to the fact
that I might someday remove it
by the drop of the kitchen cleaver
without a thumb a hand is less a hand

They tense up sometimes
as though they need something
to do as though they might
rise flapping from my lap
like wings of restless birds

On elevators I am afraid
they will go to someone's throat
in sleep I keep them jammed
between my thighs and awakening
often in the dark soak them
long in the bathroom sink
the coldest water turning them blue
each finger a fish jerking
on its hook.

The Tower

He has spent another night
walking through waves of nausea,
balancing the pain behind his eyes
to keep it from falling
through the roof of his mouth
and out onto the rug,
showing itself to be the walnut
he pictures growing
in a fold of his brain.

His coveralls will make him
a keeper of the grounds, intent
on doing battle once again
with the filthy brood of pigeons
that has called the height its own.

He will set up housekeeping in the air,
above the campus, where the tower's view
of Texas is grand and clean.

A footlocker, salvaged from a tour of duty
still active in his mind, will contain
provisions for the rest of his life:
ammunition to last the day, rimmed
by canned meats and fruit
and a rolled towel standing white
beside a spray deodorant.

In the shade given back by the wall,
he will lay three pistols, empty
and cracked open, next to a pair of rifles
soothed in oil, their telescopes hanging
ready in leather sacks.

He will give what he has to give
to anyone in sight,

completing the lives of fourteen strangers
and changing the color of August
for the dozens left to bleed.

When it is finished,
when his captors unfurl his towel
and wave it above his death,
he will join those dead as they rise
from their scarlet shadows
toward a dream he sent his women to:

Where the broken bodies of mother and wife
will mend themselves and drift in clouds,
whispering their love for him,
their fingers longing to soothe his brow
still barbed in pain.

Ward Seven, Bed Three

John rocks in his steel crib
and remembers the battle plan
that lost him his legs
and arms and voice.

John writes with a bulk-pencil
strapped to his chin.

John wanted pity at first, then
John wanted love, then
John wrote his ex-boss asking
for the position of Chief
paperweight.

John has a page-turner now;
better than the nose-method
he'd used for the first five
years; it was donated.

John listens to the volunteers
for just so long these days,
and then burrows his head
under the pillow, and comes up
waving a small American flag
between his teeth.

A Room With a Bath

He sat in the tub, dry
in his undershorts, his
shirt and trousers neat
on the toilet lid

A new blade in the soap
dish, a can of Drano
in his left hand

On top of the faucets
the bread knife he had
bought that afternoon

He reached a bathroom glass
and filled it half full
of Drano, added all
the water it would take
and stirred it well
with his finger

He drank it down
and nine times
put the knife into
his belly, next
the razor each wrist
often

He left a trail to the hall
where he crawled for help
to live to die again.

Bed

He has taken to weeping
while finding his way
back to his room.

By noon he curls up
in a knot and squints
himself to sleep
for the rest
of the day.

Sometimes he has toast
and milk before bed
so he won't wake up
in the afternoon.

Often he showers
before drawing the shades
and removing the phone
from its cradle.

Once, unable to sleep,
he scrubbed the floor
with a washcloth.

Last Tuesday, a man told him
no one would ever hire
anyone who wore a sweater
under his sport coat.

Yesterday, a man swore
he would hire him
within the year; he even
put his name in his desk.

But they can all read his face;
it tells them what they know

already: he has gone too long;
they are right in turning him
back to the street.

At Midnight

He saw the cardinal,
perched like a fist of blood,
fall through his mind
to the ground
where the girl's body
worked with the wind
to form a curled drift
that kept the river
from rising to claim her.

She lay as though in bed,
one arm bent across her brow,
the moon shading her lips
and left shoulder.

Puffs of snow
had settled on her eyes
like gobs of cotton
younger girls use
to shield their lids
at summer shores.

She was nude,
save a stocking
the color of sun-tanned legs
knotted
around her neck
much the way she might
have worn a scarf.

Her hair
flecked with night snow
was frozen to the skin
of a bulging root.

Kneeling to learn her face,
he found only frost, and rose
to dress her warm
in a garment of green branches.

The Circuit

The chapel doors are chained
and the parents cannot get at the poet
to stop him from reading to their daughters
who have rented him for the afternoon.

One woman swears she saw him
carrying a suitcase crammed with poems,
some sticking out of the corners
like underwear.

The parents have rimmed the building
and pound it with their fists,
growing louder by the hour; and now
the stained glass windows are crashing
open with borrowed books and shoes;
but the poet will not stop reading.

The coeds climb one another
to shield the poet who wants to read
his whole valise of poems.

Parents have reached the ledges
and are poking at their daughters
who moan in unison,
straining to hear the poet.

He goes on for still another hour and stops.
He packs his poems and puts on his hat;
he steps to the nearest window
where a girl smiles and opens her legs for him;
he wraps his arms around his poems
and crawls through her before dropping
to the lawn where he waits for the parents

To notice; they do and beat on him
until he opens his case

and gives them each a poem; there are not enough
and he takes out pads of yellow paper
and squats at their feet, writing more poems
that are snatched away.

The first readers are finished
and rip the poems into flakes
that settle about him like moths;
they want more, and he writes them

While their daughters take turns
putting their fingers in his mouth,
their bodies writhing in ecstasy
as they feel the movement of letters
closing into words.

On Attending a Lecture on Cruelty

On Attending a Lecture on Cruelty

The one on our right is tuxedoed;
the other is wrapped in a sling of burlap,
pinned low at the hip; both are bald,
neither is tanned, though summer is just over;
most certainly they are brothers.

On a stretch of bamboo, some well-used
paraphernalia: a two-foot run
of garden hose, a larger cut
of steel rod, the antique thumbscrew
seen in the advertisements,
& a helmet, its iron straps
crossing like the weave of a basket.

At the back wall of the stage, hung
in black scrims, are four shapes;
nothing is said of them,
but we do learn from the diapered twin
that the brother is mute;
we respond with applause, & the mute
bows, extending his hand to his brother
who affixes the thumbscrew & leads
him to the footlights.

He asks the front row
to note the pressure of wood on bone;
it is a young woman who winks
at her companion & stands,
giving the knob an extra turn; we stomp
& whistle for the mute
who is dancing on one foot, trying
to loosen the screw that squeaks
in its socket; he tosses it off

to the lady who presses it hard
to her lips.

His brother is calling him back
to center stage where he is struck
on the swelling thumb, across both thighs,
the face & top of head, the hose
leaving welts to last the matinee.

He limps upstage, smoothing away
his bruises, & removes
the first black cloth; we see
a roughshod contraption of four legs,
a comical horse's head
& a backbone too sharp for sitting;
we are told it is The Timber Mare
of dungeon days.

The mute drops his pants, & mounts,
awaiting his brother's climb;
we admire his pain, & clap till our palms sting,
his brother balancing & leaping up
& down on the mute's pale shoulders.

If he could make a sound,
it would be now, but nothing comes
from the open mouth, and it is over;
he is on one leg again, pulling
his trousers on, as his brother skips
to the second cloth, giving us
The Rack, its huge wheel glistening
like a spool of thread used up.

The mute is fitted to the bottom ropes
& cuffed to those above; he is
asked questions of faith, & nods

his head in answer, but none will do; the stomach
skin stretches, the jacket slides
up, the shirttail comes out;
but the brother is tired of turning the stile;
the ropes sag, the mute slumps,
the curtain falls.

We hurry to the lobby
where the twins have promised to mingle, & find
the mute somehow refreshed, the other,
sullen against a wall, promising more
than our money's worth once
back in our seats.

II

The houselights blink & the performers
leave through a side door to the alley, the mute
patting the other's back, trying
to lift his spirit, but he'll have none of it.

The stage looks the same; there are
new costumes; the mute:
leather trousers & vest, mountain boots
laced on hooks. The other wears faded dungarees.

Falanga is first—the steel rod glitters
in the mute's gloved hand, & already
it is clear his brother
is a poor sport; seated on one chair,
he complains as his feet are forced into the slats
of another; the soles face us.

The mute begins by tapping, but now
he is whipping, studiously,

the rod whirring in the air, the brother
biting his tongue, waiting it out; we count twelve
strokes; the mute dislodges the feet,
& the brother stays put,
soles too puffed to stand.

Beneath the third cloth is The Chair,
four-wheeled & homemade, its power drawn
from the car battery bolted to its side, two clamps
as large & as red as needle-nosed pliers
are attached to the skin of the Adam's apple
& the slight roll of fat at the waist.

The mute flicks on the head-high electrometer,
with numerals large enough to see, & from behind
The Chair, he eases a dial from zero to nine;
the brother glares above us; twenty
gets a jump, back to twelve, up to thirty-five;
the brother braces himself, pants for breath
when he sinks to ten, & is jerked from his seat
when the needle hits fifty & falls; his curse
tells the mute he has gone too far; he
reminds him of the evening ahead on The Rack.

The Helmet is a thumbscrew for skulls,
& the brother adjusts it to size, his spirit
lighter, explaining the headaches pagans
were given; the mute smiles & takes a card
from his vest, unfolding it for all to see
its word: Excedrin; we applaud as he tightens
the nut with a common wrench.

The brother has said "enough" four times,
but the mute is turning toward his own idea
of enough, & the brother pulls

at The Helmet, letting words fly unrehearsed
through the darkened theatre.

Now the mute glides to the last cloth,
removing it as one might take a shawl
from a birdcage, & it is that, exactly: a huge
barred cage, the padlock hanging open
on its ring; how strong the mute must be;
he has his brother in his arms, like a child,
knees to face, arms pinned; he sticks him
in the cage & secures the door.

There is much complaining, begging the mute
to remove The Helmet, but the mute is fumbling
with a switch; the cage starts to revolve,
its turntable gaining momentum, as a music,
heard often at carnivals, flows to the ear.

The mute is bowing & clapping, leading us all
in applause, stopping to point at the brother,
as a conductor points at a star; spinning,
spinning, the merry-go-round tune
too loud to hear; we rise to our feet,
as the curtain descends, the lights come on,
& souvenirs go on sale in the aisle.

Those Mourned

Blizzard

The drift he slams into swallows the hood;
he rams the gearshift into reverse and listens
to the tires burning themselves bald, the wind
sealing the road behind; there's no going back.

He turns off the ignition and laughs; already
late for supper, he allots two hours for the plow
to make its way to this back road he took at whim,
another test of his mettle; every day more proof
piling up, giving him strength to go on,
surviving on memory alone.

Forty, greying, he stuffs his pants cuffs inside
his socks, zips his jacket to the throat
and slips on his racing gloves, the leather
matching his leftover tan as it shows through
the patterned holes; he steps out into the snow,
knowing what to do:

The trunk opens easily, the tiny bulb giving
light enough to work; he unscrews the spare tire
and lays it flat on the roof, talking to it,
explaining what it must become, his pleasure
more proof helping to ward off the trace of panic
he knows drifts like a shadow at the edge of the road.

The sun visor breaks off neatly, making a scoop
to scatter the snow from the hood; he opens it
and unhooks the gas filter cup; he carries it off,
chuckling, pleased, stumbling ahead to the dashboard
where he shoves in the lighter and waits for it
to pop.

He pours the fuel on some crumpled paper and pokes
the orange-coiled lighter at the center of the tire,

pulling back at the whoosh of flame; he controls
the fire: large enough to warm the inside of the car,
small enough to conserve the burnables he has piled
on the front seat: glove compartment maps, credit card
tissues, six or seven old lists, a driver's manual,
last night's newspaper, and two man-sized Kleenex
he stuffed in his pocket at home this morning.

Already proud, his lips twitch as he realizes
there are yards of cardboard lining any car's
insides; he thinks of the look his insurance man
will have on his straight-lipped face when he sees
the car in the morning, destroyed for salvation;
the papers will surely do a story, pictures, quotes.

He dismantles both headlights, leaving their wires
attached, and props them in the snow, aimed skyward,
and gets back in the driver's seat flicking them on:
high low off on, a perfect signalling system for any
snowmobilers roaring drunk through virgin drifts
laced with fence posts and abandoned jalopies;

He knows the papers will set his next move in bold
type; off comes the oil filter, on goes the lubricant:
face, hands, back of neck, deep into both ears,
explaining aloud to tomorrow's reporters the need
for layers of oil, how vulnerable the hairless human
ear is to chill, the fragile pink fading to swollen
grey, yellowish white.

He sees a quarter-page photograph of himself
in a ridiculous hospital gown, pillowed-up in bed,
smiling faintly to his left; again the visor
shoveling snow high against the wind, leaving only
his door open a crack to keep the lock from freezing;
back inside he flicks on the dome light and breaks

The rearview mirror with pliers, close at the edge
so it splinters, giving him three thin blades
to strip the ceiling, allowing the tire's heat
to come in; he slashes holes in the back seat,
enough for feet and hands, another for shoes
and socks; he waits until he warms, pleased
with everything he's done.

But he knows there must be more to do; he studies
every inch of his room, trying for the extra touch
that will give the newspaper boys a headline,
a handle for a feature; he smiles and begins ripping,
wielding the glass like a scalpel:

Floor mats, lining, seat covers—and fashions a suit
of clothes: mittens and hat, scarf and shawl, pants,
boots, all jammed full of seat stuffing, tied loose
with seat belts and shoelaces; he will explain he was
about to make a pair of snowglasses out of the back
directional cups but they found him too soon.

He dresses and goes outside, removing his hand-guards
to feed the fire another slab of cardboard, recalling
the way he dropped envelopes by the dozen
into the corner mailbox three weeks ago, almost late
but close enough for Christmas; close enough
is the way he likes it, always has.

He refuses to look at his watch; he knows
it has all taken too long—clever but not clever
enough to take up the slack between the car and plow;
he curses the driver perched on his stool in some
two-bit diner, sipping coffee spoiled with milk,
a greasy doughnut ringing his finger, his boots
running snow, puddles forming on the linoleum,

streams wider than the shoelaces binding his leggings,
twisting toward the door, urging him up and out.

He hears him brag on about the weather, the way
he blasts it off the roads, how he's beaten his own
record already: only five back roads to go,
and the snow coming so fast he may forget about them
and start over from the beginning—no one in his
right mind would travel those others on such a night
anyhow.

He tastes a second cup of coffee hot in the back
of his brain, trying to suck it down; he moves his eyes
to the rearview mirror, hoping he is wrong,
planning to see the glaring lights of the plow picking him out
of the night, but he sees only a few flakes of glass left
on the flat tin backing.

He leaps within himself, remembering the car top,
clawing the air toward the tire, finding its blaze
dead, its ashes wet and done for; he gets back
in the front seat, turns the key hard to the right,
hears a rattle and remembers the hood wide open,
the motor, the battery covered with snow; he says
nothing, but takes the tire down from the roof
and puts it back in the trunk, still open, its snow
swirling up at him.

He decides to leave the headlights where they are
and gets back inside, locking the door behind him;
piece by piece by piece he pushes all the stuffing
he can find back into place, regretting the damage
he's done to the cushions and walls and ceiling.

He sits behind the wheel, and for the first time
becomes aware of snow leaking in where the vent latch
is gone; within the hour, frost starts forming
on his cheek, flakes fall on his left shoulder, the bulb
overhead continues to fade.

With fingers strangely warm, he pulls the headlight knob
and lowers his foot to the pedal: on-off, on-off,
imagining the beams changing their tilt
somewhere beneath the snow.

Cook-Out

I rise from the sun-deck
to enter the thicket
in search of a bouncing ball,
and find instead a grenade
rolling toward a thatched hut.

And I go deep within it:
my eyes dropping to a sling,
hung from criss-cross poles,
supporting a child, sleeping
above the settling ball.

The concussion blows the roof off
like a puff of dandelion fuzz:
gently, not to waken the infant
wrapped in flame and floating
slowly, head over heels through leaves.

I watch until he burns away in the sun.

An Office with a View

A man just died under my nose;
he sat down on the pavement
eleven stories below
and tried to hold his heart
in place, as I leaned out
to watch him die, careful
to clutch the sill
so I wouldn't beat him
to death in mid-air.

I closed the blinds,
but not in time to keep
his wife and children
from screaming
in the center of my desk.

Reunions

The dead rise in memory to fix
their eyes on rooms gone empty
without them; they swell like balloons
on the airy lips of children.

They will find you alone, at night,
seated in darkness; say nothing
save their names; no greeting,
no words of disbelief, only the names.

They will sense your trust,
taking the breath from the walls,
tasting the carpet for salt
left from the tears you spilled.

You will hear them behind the chair,
parting the fabric, arranging themselves
in the stuffing, sitting atop one another
in your position; the slightest pressure
beneath your legs, against your back,
will tell you they are there.

Speak their names soothingly, time
and again; by dawn you will feel
frantic motion and then nothing at all.

Turn all lights on; open all windows;
look for the yellow taint of heat,
the slight marks where the cloth
has been fused.

On the third day, inscribe a thin cross
on the seat cushion, and burn the chair
where it stands, intoning the names
as softly as your voice allows; watch
for shapes in the flame, in smoke.

Only then will you see them clearly,
bursting a moment beyond recognition.

The Bequest

He once dreamed of burning this house
    rather than bicker with his sisters
    over the relics of her life.

But she had her way, as mothers do,
    and he followed her shadow
    through endless rooms

All the while digesting the words
    that described the last remains
    her daughters must share with him

Like mice sniffing their larder
    in darkened pantries;
    there's a hutch

For a breezeway, the dry-sink
    for a cluttered kitchen floor,
    a kidney-desk and wing chair

Waiting like tombstones
    to crowd a pitiful living room;
    the spoolbed, the sleighbed

The chest of drawers ready to warp
    and flake in the rafters
    of a desolate garage.

When she's gone, they'll be back
    to handle things
    and claim her

Lefthand diamond, to lock the house
    and remove those
    crystal doorknobs.

One-Eleven Grape Street

("My clock is down at the jeweler's and I don't know when to eat or
when to go to bed or get up, but anyway I live on and on and on.")

She was eager to be heard and nibbled on memories,
while I listened to the mournful chewing, and
scraped the last puddle of vanilla ice cream
from a deep-bottom dish with a silver-black spoon.
The wool-wrapped legs barely showed but bulged
beneath uncountable layers of arctic skirts
safety-pinned each day against the imaginary freeze.
There were always cookies in the pickle crock
and Pepsi in jelly jars during those hours together
in that fear-fed neighborhood on the fringe of Lake Erie.

I remember her padding blindly about,
in her frayed maroon slippers, pressing dustballs
and giant hairpins into the silent carpet;
a copper-colored gas heater pumped itself year 'round,
and the temperature held to its constant eighty-five,
having leapt there once many years before.
The sun would sear its way through two paper shades
that were drawn and tacked against the eternal glare,
as I'd read to her from the accumulated mail,
a slim stack forever staling in open envelopes.

And then the men came—
they tapped at the windows,
took the tacks from the shades,
broke the ice cream bowls,
hid her slippers,
unpinned her skirts,
stole her mail,
and sat on the table-top to taunt her.
Only finger-tip tall, they were never seen,
but she assaulted them daily, fiercely.
In the end, they went away, leaving her alone
with the fear that they might return.
She died in her sleep without them.

The Veteran

Those eyes refused to stay indoors;
instead, they rode their own cataracts
and washed ashore at the foot
of San Juan Hill in time to watch
eighteen hundred men lace their boots
in Grandma's darkened sunporch.

From my vantage point
on Great Uncle's lap, I heard
General Shafter address his troops
and lead the attack.

Uncle Steve followed him and left me
alone in the lowlands,
already cluttered with legs
of understanding relatives
and a green hassock, frayed but firm
enough for a warrior's foothold.

Grandmother took my hand
and hurried out of the war zone,
as Uncle Steve ranted on and rode off
into combat somewhere near the front
door shining with its double lock
of inescapable security.

Old Drummer in the Poorhouse

There is no hi-hat, but he finds one
in the air around his knees
and keeps the offbeat
while his supper tray jiggles on his lap,
taking the beating he gives it
with crossrods from two wooden hangers.

They keep him downstairs
so those wrapped in silence
along the upper walls won't complain
about paradiddles accompanied
by the rudimentals of ma-ma-da-da
and the barefooted thud tap thud,
thud tap thud, of a man
at work.

A radio drifts in from the ward
overhead, and wood takes on straw
as clothesbrushes move across plastic,
scratching a chee-chaa from the thirties.

He watches his face in waves of glass
and smiles through stubble; he sees
his nursemaid swallow her laughter
and tuck him back to bed
to watch his life spin across the ceiling
and down the wall, finding itself
again in the cracked and shadowed
mirror.

Handing Over the Cabin

An hour, maybe two, was all he had
before he left; he wouldn't look
at any of the things he'd made
from dreams before it all went bad.

He wanted to know:
would we replace the wooden icebox;
might the cabin become another house;
were we able to close a place for winter.

He taught us to cut limb-poles
big around as an upper arm,
and prop them in under joists,
over the main floor beam, to keep
the roof from caving in.

We learned to make shutters
for the drifting snow, and how to nail
higher windows shut against hunters
looking for a stopping place.

We wouldn't have thought of mothballs
for the floors to ward off mice,
or antifreeze for the sinks & bowls & tank,
or screening for the drain hose
where bugs swarm throughout the fall.

Before he left, he pointed out the spot
where we might chain our own canoe
upside down under the cabin,
where it would wait dry for the lake
until it finally thawed somewhere in spring.

The Outing

Newton, Mass., April 20: Five women ranging in age
from 80 to 96 drowned this afternoon when a driverless
car rolled across a rest home lawn and sank in Crystal
Lake.—NEW YORK TIMES

It was more like a dream than an ending,
the lawn chairs adrift on the grass,
the elm trees parting politely
so that ladies kept waiting might pass
before Bartlett returns from the pantry
where he's won some affection at last.

They enter the lake without Bartlett,
and settle down in the sand;
the windows are closed, except Bartlett's,
the handle comes off in the hand;
and Bartlett goes right on romancing,
knowing that they'll understand.

They sit as they sat as they waited
for Bartlett in fine livery
who's taking them all Sunday driving
and bringing them back for tea,
but Bartlett has conquered some virtue
and lingers inside wistfully.

And now though he's diving to find them,
and even holds open the door,
there is little to say of his sorrow
as he floats them each back to the shore
where the others have come to verandas
to see the five ladies once more.

An Earlier Summer than This

We'd hitch out from town,
over the bridge and across
the island's baking dust to the dockside
tavern where we'd see,
through rusted screens, the same lost men
bent at the bar, their day's ration
of coins spilled before them.

They'd watch us strip to our trunks
on the pier, plastered
with no-swimming signs, cursing
our miserable youth to themselves,
treading their way toward dusk,
a swallow at a time.

A riverboat of sorts was marooned there,
a hideout for rats, but we'd take over
the second deck, standing three-high
on each other and topple as one
into the dark Niagara, coming up
draped in garlands of slime.

Adrift in memory is that faceless man
who set aside his beer
and mumbled onto the dock to climb
to the highest tier.

We knew the black water
like the inside of our mouths:
the cable-locks and every underwater
point where holding-piles grew
like stunted oaks.

We yelled our warnings and watched
him leap, tumbling like a bag of bones.

He hit six inches of water,
forty foot of wood, hooked somehow
by the seat of his pants,
like a bar rag ready to be wrung out
and carried back inside
where it belonged.

The Plumber

He hanged himself last night
    quiet in his own cellar
    while his wife tidied up
    the kitchen overhead.

She called his name softly,
    aware of the pain
    that had hung in his head
    since the fall last spring.

She called a second time
    and dried both hands
    on her apron as she pattered
    down the stairs to find him

Swaying from a nylon cord knotted
    hard against the sewer pipe;
    he must have stood there
    silent on his toolbox

And kicked himself free, plunging
    feet first into darkness,
    flushing the ache from his life
    like a house-moth caught

In the swirl of a bathroom bowl.

An Ending

The papers report
that you have been found
drifting and bobbing
fifteen days downstream
from where you broke
the November silence
and slipped
from no one's sight.

Heavy with death
you rose from the riverbed,
layers of fish parting
to allow your passage
through their gaze
before giving you up
to the eyes of a man
facing his Sunday alone
along the shore.

You are landlocked now
in dry clothes and candlelight
close to those you leave
to drown
in the wake of your going.

Tomorrow, the hole in the Hudson
will heal.

For a Cook Probably Gone by Now

Arnie, you were just too short
for your own good;
nothing could make you tall:
not the extra heels nailed
drunkenly to both shoes, hidden
by dungarees dragging the floor,
your chef's hat rising a foot
overhead, that bowery face
somehow always in pain,
those snakes curling their ink
the length of your arms; nothing,
not even the milk crates
you walked like a bridge
in front of the stoves, tending
the burners like a man
too tall for such a bend;
nothing did anything, Arnie,
but remind us that the inches
you mourned were somewhere
beyond that mountain
hell-hole of pots and pans
where you always came up short.

The Elders

When death comes, it will find them
here where we tucked them away
like used kleenex, she in one wing
he in the darker, she to a suite
of carpets and drapes and her name
on the door, giving a confusion of home.

His room is as grey as mouseskin,
the warped linoleum adding only
a trim of blue-black flowers
to the bottoms of walls;
the windows are sealed
yet the screens are intact
in this ward for the terminally ill.

Her hair has been cut
to suit the fashion of the place;
the clothes she came in
have been washed and laid to rest
on a shelf she can't quite reach;
she obeys like the others
and wears the pantsuits she found
swaying on velveteen hangers
in her closet of gold-rimmed mirrors.

His wardrobe is his own:
the same flannel shirt tucked
in dark green trousers, the
cigarette hole at the crotch
still light around the rim.

She eats her meals on her side
of things, with plush pile chairs
and tin chandeliers and fourteen
plastic flowers all in a row.

He dines at the end of his hall,
raising his hand for service
or a push to the lobby to meet her,
his slippers dragging ahead
of the wheels.

She has permission to leave
her sector to join him, and does
most days, taking her place
at his side, where they wait
watching the door.

Whatever You Say, Henry

He feels the catheter as penis,
is pleased with its sudden growth,
and goes to great lengths fondling
what he can't raise his head to see;
"Pinocchio" says I; and the urine
trickles to its holding bag.

In a haze that won't describe itself,
he sees the bottles above his head,
and wonders what good they do;
"Oil change" says I; and the drops
fall to his arm and in;
"Smart Ass" says he; "You bet yours"
says I, and the toes of one foot
move the sheet in pleasure.

They like him here; like his bark,
the way he tells them why
they feel so smug, well enough
to baby him, reminding them
they'll be in a crib some day;
"Time's coming" says he.
"Whatever you say, Henry—whatever."

"Damn right" says he. Cancer or no,
he says it out: the chaplain on rounds,
gold watch and fob and vest,
comes puffing in to ask How-are-you-doing-
today-Henry? "Dying, thank you" says he.
What-is-your-line-of-work-Henry?
"English professor" says he. Oh-I'd-
better-watch-what-I-say, he says. "All
self-conscious people say that" says he.
Well-have-a-nice-day, he says.
"Amen" says he.

He still has his own mustache, and wants
to know what the plastic one does; "Oxygen
without the tent" she sings; "Enjoy it
like a breath of spring."—"Awful" says he.
"Behave" she says. "Beat it" says he.
"Please leave for a while" she says;
"I want to do his bedsores."—"Live it up"
says I. "Smart Ass" says he. "Yours,
at the moment" says I. "Bet yours" says he;
and she rolls him off his rubber ring.

        The lounge is empty, the magazines
older than a barbershop's; nothing
changes—faces smile and frown, open
and close; gossip and death survive.

Now he is propped on his side, his rump
healing in open air; the phone
rings from Alaska; the voice is hard
to place, but her name makes the catheter
jump on its hook. "She doesn't know"
says he; "It's been years."—"I'll write her"
says I. "Leave her be" says he. "Like hell"
says I; he shakes his head
in mock dismay, and sleeps in snow

For a matter of minutes, waking
in an old dream with three women naked
on a parched lawn, holding him down
in a shallow pine box; he's cold
and yelling for help. "Why
wouldn't you come; where were you?"
"Right here; it's all right,
I'm right here." Again sleep, longer,
deep enough to send me home.

Route 59 is slurred with rain; cars dead
along the curbs; the stink of the ward
hangs on.

The clock on the mantel clangs time
and again, the phone wakens the house,
a nurse talks from his room: he's confused,
thinks he is lost, would I talk him
back to sleep, do what I can.
"It'll be okay, Henry; it's just
a dream, like the box on the lawn;
the nurses will get you blankets,
and tuck you in, get you more milk,
one of those whopping pills; let me talk
with her again; you'll sleep,
you'll see."—"My ass" says he.
"No thanks" says I; "I saw it this afternoon."

Stones

He has chosen fifteen
from the side of the track,
and now the sixteenth;
he shakes them
in his cupped hands
like a man rattling bar dice
after his money is gone.

They are all about the same:
grey, smooth, just as they were
a year ago when he'd run
four miles before breakfast
—in rain, snow, summer heat,
no matter.

He watches the runners,
different yet the same,
sweatshirts wet on their backs,
legs pounding the stones in place,
a sudden burst of speed
as they pass by, nodding his way
with the nod a newsboy gives
with change, cautiously,
making sure his fingers don't
touch your palm.

He's wanted to come here
to the grandstand, stark
in its concrete
and bolted slabs of wood,
and the stones—most of all
the stones;

He remembers how he'd fondle them,
flicking one away each time
he finished a lap, running

flatout with the last one
tight inside his fist,
keeping it, storing it away
with the others at home.

The runners are at the far bend
and coming hard—they will pass him
again, where he stands aside,
feeling the stones tumbling
in the dark
he has made of his hands.

POETRY FROM ILLINOIS

History Is Your Own Heartbeat
Michael S. Harper (1971)

The Foreclosure
Richard Emil Braun (1972)

The Scrawny Sonnets and Other Narratives
Robert Bagg (1973)

The Creation Frame
Phyllis Thompson (1973)

To All Appearances: Poems New and Selected
Josephine Miles (1974)

Nightmare Begins Responsibility
Michael S. Harper (1975)

The Black Hawk Songs
Michael Borich (1975)

The Wichita Poems
Michael Van Walleghen (1975)

Cumberland Station
Dave Smith (1977)

Tracking
Virginia R. Terris (1977)

Poems of the Two Worlds
Frederick Morgan (1977)

Images of Kin: New and Selected Poems
Michael S. Harper (1977)

On Earth as It Is
Dan Masterson (1978)